ALL ABOUT THE RODEO

RODEO BARREL RACERS

Lynn Stone

Rourke
Publishing LLC
Vero Beach, Florida 32964

www.rourkepublishing.com

Photo credits:
Front cover © Winthrop Brookhouse, back cover © Olivier Le Queinec, all other photos © Tony Bruguiere except page 11 © Kate Leigh, page 18 © Cindy Riley, page 23 © Jeff Cummings, pages 13 and 25 © Rick Hyman

Editor: Jeanne Sturm

Cover and page design by Nicola Stratford, Blue Door Publishing

Library of Congress Cataloging-in-Publication Data

Stone, Lynn M.
 Rodeo barrel racers / Lynn M. Stone.
     p. cm. -- (All about the rodeo)
 Includes index.
 ISBN 978-1-60472-392-2
 1. Barrel racing--Juvenile literature. I. Title.
 GV1834.45.B35S86 2009
 791.8'4--dc22
                                    2008018797

Printed in the USA

CG/CG

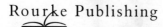

Rourke Publishing

www.rourkepublishing.com – rourke@rourkepublishing.com
Post Office Box 3328, Vero Beach, FL 32964

Table Of Contents

Barrel Racing

Barrel racing is an exciting demonstration of rodeo riding, matching a skilled rider with an equally skilled horse. It pairs highly trained, athletic horses with some of the finest riders in North America.

Barrel Racing is one of the seven main events in major rodeos. The event features a rider on a saddled horse running at breakneck speed toward, and then around, three barrels on the dirt floor of an **arena**.

Barrel racing tests the agility of both horse and rider.

The objective of a barrel racer is to guide the horse in a **cloverleaf pattern** around the triangle of barrels as quickly as possible. Like rodeo steer wrestlers, barrel racers compete only against a clock. Style does not count a lick in this event.

Horse and rider loop the barrel in a race against time.

The closer a rider can come to a barrel, the tighter a turn the horse can make. A tight turn reduces distance and time. But a tight turn also increases the risk of striking a barrel. Sometimes a horse's hoof or shoulder catches the barrel. Sometimes it's the rider's foot that nicks the barrel.

Barrel racing requires high speed and tight turns on horseback.

The idea, of course, is for the horse and rider to both avoid any contact with a barrel. The barrel will move easily, if it is hit, so it is not a particular danger.

But striking the barrel will cost the competitor. The judge will deduct five seconds from the rider's score. That is enough to assure that the ride will fall well short of a winning time.

Riders take a bigger risk the closer they come to a barrel—an overturned barrel results in a penalty.

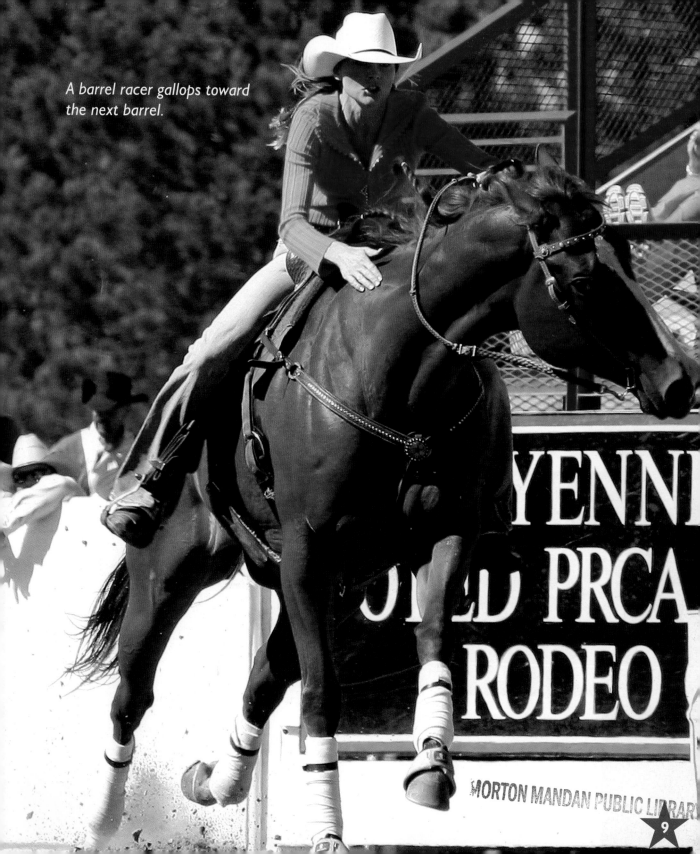

A barrel racer gallops toward the next barrel.

9

Women may well have started the sport of barrel racing. But whether or not women actually began the activity, it has **evolved** largely into a women's sport. The Women's Professional Rodeo Association (WPRA) oversees almost all the barrel races at professional rodeos, and its events are for women only. Men are not eligible to compete in barrel racing at the National Finals Rodeo.

The National Barrel Horse Association (NBHA), another governing organization, does allow men to compete in some of the events that it **sponsors**. Among professionals, however, barrel racing is essentially a women's sport.

Running the Event

The three 55-gallon (208-liter) barrels at the event are set in a triangle with two of the barrels forming a base parallel to the horse and rider's entryway to the arena. The third barrel forms the point of the triangle at an equal distance from the first two barrels.

Consider the barrels at the base of the triangle as barrel numbers 1 and 2. The point barrel, the most distant from the starting line, is barrel number 3.

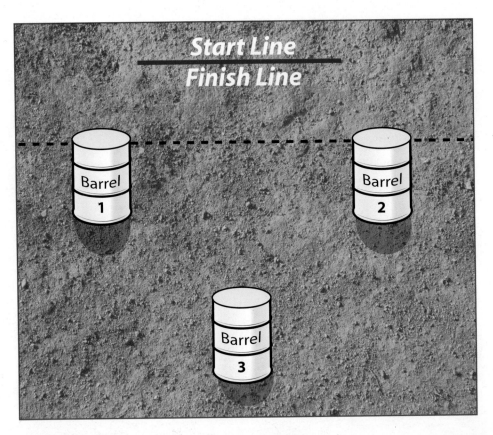

Together, the barrels make up a cloverleaf pattern.

The race begins when the rider and her horse gallop toward the arena entryway. The timer for the race begins when the two actually cross the starting line at the entry to the arena.

A rider may guide her horse toward barrel number 1 or barrel number 2. Since the distances are identical, it is a matter of the rider's choice.

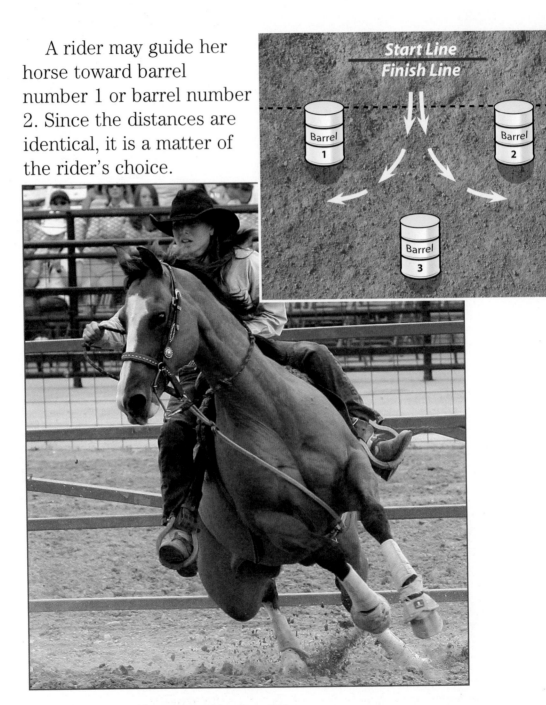

Start Line
Finish Line

Barrel 1

Barrel 2

Barrel 3

A young barrel racer bolts into the arena.

From there she will guide the horse toward the second barrel. The horse and rider will then loop barrel number 2.

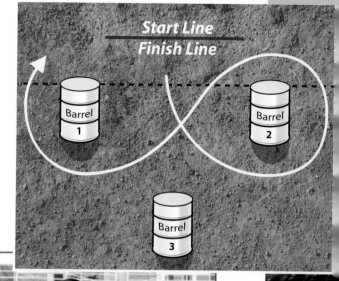

A barrel horse accelerates on course to the final barrel.

The last approach will be toward barrel number 3. The loop will bring the horse and rider back toward the base parallel and into a sprint to the starting line, which is now the finish line.

The entire race takes roughly 16 or 17 seconds, and it is timed to 1/100th of a second.

A *barrel racer leans into a tight turn around the final barrel.*

Most barrels are arranged according to a standard. The distance from the start line to either barrel 1 o 2 is 60 feet (18 meters). The distance between barrel 1 and 2 themselves is 90 feet (27 meters). The distance from barrels 1 and 2 to barrel 3 is 105 feet (32 meters). The longest sprint of the race is from barrel 3 back to the starting line. The race ends as the horse and rider dash across the finish.

Boys and girls often use junior barrel riding events to improve basic skills.

★ Each time a horse pulls into
★ a turn around a barrel, its
★ rider must be in perfect
★ position. She sits deep on
★ the saddle, keeping one hand
★ on the saddle horn. That
★ helps steady her. Her other
★ hand grips the rein to guide
★ the horse tightly around
★ the barrel.

Like any rodeo event, barrel racing is not without its perils for both the horse and the rider. Carefully fitted saddles help the rider's cause. The horse has an assist from special boots that protect its feet.

A running horse extends its two front legs forward together and its two rear legs backward together. That running motion brings the two front legs and two hind legs back together under the horse's body. That's a recipe for injury because the legs can strike each other, especially in hard turns. The boots help avoid leg injuries.

Boots protect the front legs of the horse when used in barrel racing.

The Riders

Like other successful athletes, the best barrel racers are dedicated to their sport. Good horsemanship and practice is essential, just as a good horse is essential for those who seriously pursue the sport.

Professional barrel racers compete for dollars and a variety of prizes. The best professional barrel racers win rodeo payoffs that match the payoffs of the men's events.

Barrel racers compete in pro events for prize money.

Barrel racing has no age limits. Many barrel racers begin riding as children. The National Little Britches Rodeo Association provides competition for youngsters ages 5 through 18. Young people also compete in barrel racing events sponsored by both the National High School Rodeo Association and the National Intercollegiate Rodeo Association.

The Horses

In general, horses are a mixed lot, from fleet **thoroughbreds** to mighty **draft horses**, like Clydesdales and Belgians. Barrel racing, however, requires neither the enduring speed of a thoroughbred or the might of a Clydesdale. The most popular horse in barrel racing is the American quarter horse. Quarter horses are intelligent, compact, agile, and sturdy. They are fast over short distances and can start and stop quickly.

Palomino is a coat color in horses, consisting of a gold coat and white mane and tail.

Quarter horses are often a shade of brown, but the **breed** comes in many colors, and **palomino** and **paints** are not unusual in the more typical mix of brown quarter horses.

Color does not determine the value of a barrel horse. A horse's age, condition, ancestry, and demonstrated barrel racing skills determine its value. The best of the lot sell for more than $100,000. The saddle and bit may be extra.

The History of Barrel Racing

Barrel racing probably began in Texas, possibly at the Stamford (Texas) Cowboy Reunion in 1932. Women were invited to demonstrate their horsemanship by riding in a leisurely figure eight pattern around barrels.

By the 1940s, The Cowboys Amateur Association (CAA) had begun to sponsor women's barrel racing as one of its events. The CAA was helpful to rodeo cowgirls. It held both figure eight and cloverleaf barrel racing events. The more difficult cloverleaf pattern eventually became the standard for the event.

Modern barrel racing is a much faster event than the barrel riding events of the 1930s.

Ever since rodeo's early days in the 1880s, the role of women in rodeos was limited by the men who promoted rodeos. Some women were capable and eager to participate in competitive riding events, but the women and events were few. Many rodeo promoters did not think the rodeo was a suitable place for ladies. Women riders were hired by rodeos mostly to add an element of beauty, bright costuming, and

Today, skill and speed have galloped over glamour.

glamour. The role of rodeo women was largely to ride in parades, formations, and trick riding acts.

The role of women in rodeo slowly changed. The beauty pageant element gave way to increased opportunities for serious competition among talented women who were willing to ride and work hard. Women were increasingly recognized for their ability and effort.

The role of women in rodeo events has changed to one of competition.

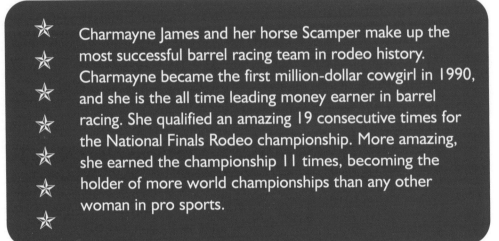

Charmayne James and her horse Scamper make up the most successful barrel racing team in rodeo history. Charmayne became the first million-dollar cowgirl in 1990, and she is the all time leading money earner in barrel racing. She qualified an amazing 19 consecutive times for the National Finals Rodeo championship. More amazing, she earned the championship 11 times, becoming the holder of more world championships than any other woman in pro sports.

The Girls' Rodeo Association (GRA), founded in 1948, gave cowgirls a much-needed organization to champion their activities. The GRA became the WPRA in 1981 as rodeo became increasingly popular.

Until recent years, barrel racing did not match men's rodeo **purses**. But that barrier has fallen, too. Professional barrel racers compete for prize money that is the equal of men's purses in other rodeo events.

Today, barrel racing is a big time rodeo event. It's in the mainstream of rodeo, and it has become one of the most popular women's sports in North America.

Glossary

arena (uh-REE-nuh): a large enclosure in which rodeo and other events are held for public view

breed (BREED): a particular kind of domestic animal within a larger, closely related group, such as the quarter horse within the horse group

cloverleaf pattern (KLOH-vur-leef PAT-urn): an arrangement of objects that has three or four points, in the manner of a three-leafed or four-leafed clover

draft horses (DRAFT HORSS-iz): horses of heavyset breeds developed for work, such as pulling wagons

evolved (i-VOLVD): having changed through a gradual process

paints (PAYNTZ): horses of either the paint breed or of a mixed color pattern that often looks like splattered paint

palomino (pal-uh-MEE-noh): not a specific breed of horse, but a horse of a cream or golden color, often with white trim

purses (PURSS-iz): prize monies

sponsors (SPON-surz): when a person or group pays to make an event happen

thoroughbreds (THUR-oh-breds): the foremost breed of racing horse

Further Reading

Want to learn more about rodeos? The following books and websites are a great place to start!

Books

Broyles, Janell. *Barrel Racing*, Rosen, 2006.

James, Charmayne. *Charmayne James on Barrel Racing,* Western Horseman, 2005.

McRae, Marlene. *Barrel Racing 101: A Complete Program for Horse and Rider,* Lyons Press, 2006.

Websites

http://www.wpra.com
http://www.charmaynejames.com
http://www.nbha.com/about/index.shtml
www.nlbra.com

Index

About The Author

Lynn M. Stone is a widely published wildlife and domestic animal photographer and the author of more than 500 children's books. His book *Box Turtles* was chosen an Outstanding Science Trade Book and Selectors' Choice for 2008 by the Science Committee of the National Science Teachers' Association and the Children's Book Council.